Jackie Hagan was raised on broken biscuits in a little town that's now studied on the GCSE syllabus as a 'failed social experiment'. She spent half of her childhood in fancy dress at a Scouse dance school and the other half engaging merrily with her eight imaginary friends. She studied philosophy at university which sent her mad.

Jackie performs poetry and comedy and doesn't quite fit into either category. She writes plays, makes 'things' and runs workshops, and for the past twelve years has run Seymour Poets, a creativity project for isolated adults based at blueSCI Arts and Wellbeing centre in Manchester. She likes the broken, the forthright, and the jumble souled.

Also by Jackie Hagan

Shut Your Eyes and Put Out Your Hand [Citizen 32]
The Wisdom of the Jumble Sale [Flapjack Press]

"Jackie Hagan is a unique and utterly compelling performer.
Her new show is a moving and darkly humorous take on
coming to terms with the bad stuff life throws at us. With wit
and charm, she manages to make us laugh in the face of
adversity."
Matt Fenton, Artistic Director, Contact Theatre

"If Jackie is available to run a workshop for you, book her -
she's brilliant, creative, inclusive, inspiring, compassionate and
inventive. In twenty years I can't say I've known anyone run
better workshops for us than Jackie."
Pete Kalu, Artistic Director, Commonword

jackiehagan.weebly.com

Some People Have Too Many Legs is the winner of
the Best Spoken Word Show at Saboteur Awards 2015
and winner of a Creative Future Literary Award 2015.

A Contact Theatre/Flying Solo/National Rural Touring Forum
commission, supported by Arts Council England
and in association with Take Art.

Jackie Hagan

Some People Have Too Many Legs

- The Script of the Show -

Flapjack Press
flapjackpress.co.uk

Exploring the synergy between performance and the page

First published in 2015 by Flapjack Press
Salford, Gtr Manchester
flapjackpress.co.uk

Revised and reprinted in 2015
Reprinted in 2016

ISBN 978-0-9932370-1-0

Front cover photo © Johnathan Clover: johnathanclover.com
Back cover photo © Lee Baxter: baxterphoto.co.uk
Cover design & illustrations © Brink: paulneads.co.uk
Page 35 photo by Rikki Beadle Blair
Page 52 photo by Miles Charles Hadderton

Printed by Imprint Digital
Upton Pyne, Exeter, Devon
imprintdigital.com

'Tea of Coffee?' was first published in
The Wisdom of the Jumble Sale [Flapjack Press, 2009]

With thanks to producer Jayne Compton, touring technician Benny Jo Zahl, support worker Simon James, Rikki Beadle Blair, Oli Sykes, Lynsey Akehurst, Byron Vincent, Mark Whitelaw, Janice Connolly, Lowri Evans, Mark Helyar at Take Art, Liz Bouch, Babs and Sara at Amputee Outreach, Dr Ian Bruce at Manchester Royal Infirmary, Professor Kulkaani, Elaine Neville, and the surgeon who cut it off.

Thanks also to Conor Aylward, Steve Lyons, Gerry Potter, Ange Middleton, Clare Shaw, Vanessa Baggot, Steph Pike, Elliot Hughes, Flo Parry, Brink, Tony Walsh, Joy France, Fergus Evans, Sophie Willan, Jez Smith, Rachel Lancaster, Felix Henson, Matt Panesh, Kieren King, Ella Gainsborough, Viney, Helen Derby, Andrea Whittaker, Kate Fox, Gina and John at 3MT, everyone who visited and posted weird stuff to me in hospital.

Mum and our Mike.

And Miles.

Dedicated to Chris Murray, 1949 - 2014.
And to the last time you stoically smiled
and kept your shit together.

In 2013 I got sick and brought down the national average number of legs, then I did a show about it.

So, without giving away too much (seeing as you are about to read the story), this is what happened: two years ago I got a commission to write a show, and then a month later I went into hospital over the road from the theatre, while I was in there I wrote about what was going on, I lost my flat when I came out because I was in a wheelchair and my flat was very high up in the sky without a lift, so while I was making and touring the show I was off my head on morphine and trauma. It won a couple of awards (I'm totally showing off now, we've gone from *X Factor* sob story to 'aren't I great' with only a full stop to give us order) and I went round selling my story to those sort of magazines your Mum reads on the toilet, and now it's *now*. So it's been a mental two years. Somehow during all that I sort of forgot to mention in the show that I'm bisexual and bipolar; I used to make a lot of work about that, and getting people to be accepting about that stuff is dead important to me. I thought about muddying up the narrative by sticking that stuff in, but instead I've stuck on a couple of poems at the start. Job's a good 'un.

The most common question people ask me is *Why did you have your leg off?* I don't answer this fully in the show because I don't know the answer and neither do the doctors. I have something called Systemic Sclerosis, but that doesn't make you lose your leg. I also have something called Raynaud's Syndrome, but to lose your leg from that is pretty rare. I also have Fuch's Syndrome, but that has nothing to do with legs (but is more fun to tell people you have). What we know is that I had a sudden, very large cluster of blood clots in the main artery in my leg. The moment this happened is the moment of mystery; there was a spasm, that is it, a mystery spasm. Scary, isn't it. So I have embraced uncertainty, eat more veg, and appreciate what I have, because you never know what's round the corner (it could be an old lady who looks like a threadbare tennis ball).

Jackie Hagan

Tea or Coffee?

I was born and they said "I bet she'll like coffee",
the right chromosomes you see and
I cared not a jot,
happy with my breast milk,
I didn't understand why everyone was so het up
about hot drinks.
But time passes and I turned twelve;
started to look at mugs,
china cups,
saw the tea my father chain drank,
the coffee my mother savoured,
figured either would do to douse my thirst.

Looked up with childish glee and saw tall faces:
"You will drink coffee,
you will admire coffee,
you will fall in love with coffee,
settle down with coffee,
you will serve coffee all your goddamn life."
Didn't think it was worth asking about tea.

So I did drink coffee.
I drank it by the gallon:
tried instant coffee against the back walls of clubs,
tried espresso, found it was over too soon,
tried filter coffee, who told me to lose weight,
tried latte which was just
too phlegmy.

Coffee was jittery,
didn't know where to put its hands,
thought it was something special if I at least enjoyed it.

Coffee was demanding:
I must wear make up and a dress!
Requested I pluck my eyebrows,
moaned about my breasts,
coffee wanted me to wank it off in the middle of the night.

Eventually I asked:
"It's alright this coffee, but have you got anything else?"

"Oh yes my dear, but it's not for you!
You like coffee remember?
Coffee fulfils you completely."

"Oh."

Kinder ones replied:
"Maybe you just haven't had the right cup of coffee yet."

But coffee was fine, it did the job,
it was hot and wet and I wasn't thirsty afterwards.

But that I'm told we mustn't do becomes just that
which we pursue
and I was surrounded
without censor
by sexy, curvy, sweet cups of tea
slurped carelessly by boys and men.

"It's not for you!"

"But my father loved tea!"

I flirted relentlessly, but knew I couldn't drink it...
didn't know *why* I couldn't drink it,
thought I'd really like to try it,

felt ashamed I'd like to try it,
couldn't help but *try* to try it.
So under the pretence of seeking a university degree
came to Manchester, in ravenous search for tea.
And tea leaks out Manchester's walls!
University life is filled with tea:
crusty dreadlocked herbal tea;
Daddy Prada Earl Grey tea;
enthusiastic new found tea with asymmetric hairdos.
There's tea meetings, shops and clubs.
There's even a tea drinkers' pub!

Tea took me,
nourished me,
let me be me,
in pyjamas, unshaven, unplucked.
Tea fucked me like tea does.
Didn't shriek at menstruation
or react with indignation when I wouldn't wank it off.
Didn't moan about my breasts, for tea has breasts too!
Went on a bit about goddesses,
but tea knew where to put its hands
and I knew how to treat tea.
And what a surprise:
tea was better at it then me!

But the world of tea it seems is not itself without restriction
for tea drinkers can't help but force the conviction
I must drink only tea!
(When they found out I'd slurped a cup of coffee
that very morning).

They said coffee was against us,
said that coffee was the enemy,

and with a exhausted sense of déjà vu
I grew sick of this dichotomy of just what it is I must not do.
And remember, that we must not do
becomes just that which we pursue
and coffee leaks out Manchester's walls!

I learnt to avoid the phlegmy coffee,
the coffee that just wanted to watch me drink tea.
Found coffee that knew where to put its hands,
and coffee took me,
nourished me,
let me be me,
in pyjamas, unshaven, unplucked,
coffee fucked me like coffee does.

But, like The Beatles and The Rolling Stones,
I mustn't admit to enjoying both
and in a quandary lived a double life,
and slowly noticed the world was rife
with those who want their coffee and their tea;
drink one in public, the other secretively.
The same who bawl with self-righteous anger
that I must choose.

Weary of hypocrites (for they protest too much)
I held up my head and took a mug,
a tea bag
and a spoonful of coffee,
and stirred
and stirred
and didn't stop
when they objected,
didn't stop
when they rejected me from tea drinking clubs.

And now,
when I drink tea
they call me a tea drinker.
When I drink coffee,
a coffee drinker.
But they know
I do both:

I drink tea, I drink coffee.
Because they both whet my whistle.

You Can't See Through Another Man's Eyelids

In here, everything's broken:
the activity cupboard's broken
the kettle's broken,
this felt tip's fucked;
just keep banging your head against the wall,
we know that works.

Come on in, it's like a holiday from life,
the view from the dayroom of men pacing
and holding it in
until they don't,
women in crazy-women coats with no hope
and sick from trying,
and we smoke a lot,
and every day at nine and twelve and five for meals
we have food,
and we smoke a lot.

Come on in, you're just in time,
Beryl's kicking off and screaming all that stuff
that we all already know
from the last time she kicked off,
with more arms and legs and tears
and the nurse's face and blood
and later
she'll come, sedated, into the dayroom,
tail tucked and shamed
that we all know
what we all know,
what we all know anyway.

Come on in, it's like an Enid Blyton boarding school
and instead of matron
we've got Elaine the nurse
who's going grey too early from empathy
and no time to care,
and Lucy the young nurse
on whom it's just dawning
that this system
doesn't work.
But once a week we have ward round
and it's all straighteners and bobbles
and Beth thinks she might get a chance to go home.
And we wait

and wait

and

wait

until the Lord our Saviour,
the psychiatrist,
is ready to look at us with his peripheral vision -
with his surprising lack of interpersonal skills
considering he's chosen to work with people and psyches.
You see, some psychiatrists need to learn one sentence;
when someone tells you something horrific
that's happened to them,
which they will cos you ask them
again and again,
just say this:

"I'm really sorry that happened to you."

(The set resembles a child's blanket fort, a hospital ward and a cosy circus freak show. There are teddies with one leg cut off sat in the audience. Jackie wears striped pyjamas)

My name is Jackie Hagan and I am not a proper grown up; I can't put a duvet cover on without getting stuck inside, I still don't eat my crusts and I live off crisp butties and the validation of strangers. The thing is, I've never wanted to be one, I never saw the appeal, until now. You see, this is a bit embarrassing, but I want to impress this lad - Miles Charles Hadderton. He's a proper grown up, an Oxford graduate; says words like 'integral' and 'tarragon' and 'life insurance', drinks red wine instead of Um Bongo and vodka, grows his own herbs and thinks that's normal - and has reluctantly agreed to be my boyfriend (my particular brand of flirting is a delicate balance of push-up bras and bullying).

The thing is, I don't think he's completely sold on me, he knows I'm chaos, he knows I spent my twenties in and out of psychiatric wards. I tried to reassure him, I told that I've not been there for ages - in fact, the last time I was there was that special time in British history, you know, that summer when Jedward came into our lives. They were everywhere, in magazines, on telly, and I was nuts, so I thought Jedward was a symptom of my psychosis. I thought I'd made that shit up!

Those first two months with Miles were anxious bliss. We went to the theatre, we went to the cinema, we went to A+E.

They kept me in.

[F/X: Hospital monitors 'beep' in the background]

I hate hospitals, they're so beepy! It's like living in a techno album that doesn't know how to dance. I've been in this little room for hours. This room does not want to be a room anymore, it stinks of TCP and disabled cliché. And the pain! I've never known pain like it! It's like learning there is a new colour! But shite.

Plus... I don't know if it's all the morphine, but every time the doctor comes he's got a different head. I'd never learn all the names; Dr Smith, Dr Jones, Dr Frankenstein! But I remembered something my Dad taught me when I was growing up:

"What do you do if you don't know something? Make it up."

* * *

"Hello Dr Dre!"

The doctor tells me that I've got a massive cluster of blood clots in my main artery in my ankle, there's stuff that they can do and none of it sounds good, but it's important to endure cos it might save my legs and my life.

Save my legs?

Save my life?!

"Miss Hagan, if we do this blaah blaaah procedure you might not die."

Might not die?

Might NOT die.

I might not die! I might be... immortal!

Well, I've always suspected.

[F/X: Background noise of a busy pub, with 'Too Much Too Young' by The Specials playing on the Jukebox]

The Dog and Gun pub is rammed. Twenty-eight years before the smoking ban and they're smoking like they know it's coming. This is the type of pub that does quality meat raffles, where there's always a terrier lapping beer from an ashtray, and you don't sit in *that* seat! *That's* ald Tommy's seat!

There's a gang of lads because there's always a gang of lads. One of them, a dirty blond with an Irish twang is wearing a green jumper; he grips the ends of his sleeves so his feelings don't fall out and pretends to be taller. He's seventeen, for the past fifteen minutes he's been trying to make eyes at The Girl. This pub is full of girls, girls with long brown hair and outfits they think the boys will like, but *this* girl? This girl is unapologetically her. She's sixteen but she knows a thing or two, an enthusiastic name on the nightclub scene, one night she's a mod, the next night she's rocking, but tonight - she's a go-go dancer in silver boots and a black bobbed wig. She could steal any girl's boyfriend, she's not perfect though, she's just... something.

"Hey! Green Jumper! I'm not willing to wait all night for yer!" she lies. Before he knows it she's up in his face, her breath smells of snakebite and black. She wants to tell him he's got beautiful eyes, instead she drunkenly drags him outside.

[F/X: Background pub noise stops]

The shock of cold, she pulls his arms around her and whispers truthfully, "I've chosen you."

And, nine months later, I'm born.

* * *

If you're a good Catholic you're meant to name your child after a saint, so they named me after one of *Charlie's Angels*.

The waiting list for a council flat in them days was as long as the Mersey Tunnel, so we were living in my Dad's teenage bedroom until something miraculous happened: Liverpool decided to build a promised land...

[F/X: Fanfare]

called Skelmersdale.

Skelmersdale! A new town with one shop and a bus stop with half a can of lager in it.

Skelmersdale! Fifteen miles from anything of use or interest!

Skelmersdale! Loads of cheap housing no one else wants!

Skelmersdale!

... Skem.

My Mum sits at the dining room table all day with loads of little bits of shammy leather which she glues together to make one big shammy leather for 12p a go, but in her head, she's dancing on a podium.

My Dad gets a job far away. At the weekend I'd count the cuts on his hands. I make him little presents, like, I don't like the nut ones in Revels so I suck the chocolate off and at the weekend I present him with a little pile of peanuts.

The whole house reeks of superglue and hard graft. When I grow up, I want to live in a house that doesn't smell of glue, so I have a plan - when I grow up I will be clever. When I grow up I will be... a duck trailer!

(A duck trailer is someone who follows the duck footprints in the snow and finds the duck at the other end. Duck trailers do not exist.)

Scene 4

[F/X: Hospital monitors 'beep' in the background]

When you're sick you get loads of attention! My mates have decorated the wall behind my bed with the best headlines from the worst magazines: 'A ghost sat my Geography A-levels', 'I hide biscuits underneath my giant boobs', 'My toddler has a spray tan', 'I run over my dog and now he walks sideways like a crab'.

The woman in the next bed is called Edna, she's seventy-two and she looks like a threadbare tennis ball with eyes. She hates Mancs, Scousers, coffee, tea, swearing, toddlers, wisdom, jumble sales, Noel Edmonds, my tattoos, my hair, my face, me, and above all, nurses. I love Edna! She's got balls, I can imagine her in leather.

On the other side is Sally. I cannot imagine Sally in leather. She likes jam and gin, and is one of those people who's kept her life in a biscuit tin. She lies on her side, her eyes are big and bewildered like a cow.

"Nurse! Nurse! Nurse!"

The nurses ignore her and this pisses me off, so I flop over to see what she wants. She wants me to tickle her on the back! It is big and spongy and the temperature of rice pudding, just at the point the skin forms. Once I've done it, she asks me again. I tickle her big expanse of a back seven times, and then I start ignoring her, too.

[F/X: The theme tune to *Button Moon* plays quietly in the background]

When I was three I was obsessed with the raindance -

"AHAHAHAHAHAHA!"

And then my Mum told me that there's another one called the sundance, which is exactly the same, only silent.

When I was four my parents took me to the set of *Brookside* (if you're too young to remember *Brookside*, it was basically a Scouse *Coronation Street* only with more patios and lesbians) and I was made-up, and then years later I found out that you can't go to the set of *Brookside*, my parents had just taken me to a cul de sac.

When I was five my hamster died and I asked my Mum, "Is this going to happen to me? Am I going to die?" and my Mum said, "No." My Mum said that my entire family are immortal because we'd been chosen specifically by Noel Edmonds.

My parents were dead ordinary but sort of bonkers from having kids too young, too poor, and too Skem, so I was brought up on love, lies, spam, optimism and imagination. But in me that's more pronounced cos I have something wrong with my eyes genuinely called 'Fuch's Syndrome'. It means there's more glare from lights - I'm like a cross between a mogwai and a pensioner.

One time, I was on a replacement bus service from Liverpool to Manchester (living the dream) and it was one of them nights where the moon is full and fat and satisfying - one of them nights when you want to go and live in the woods - and I've always had these kind of panic attacks from happiness, when I see something beautiful it makes me all breathy and mental (the first time I ever had one of these happy attacks was when I was little and I first saw a tombola) and no one on this bus was looking at this moon, they were all looking at their phones, so in this mental breathy way I got them all to look out the window: "LOOK AT THE BEAUTIFUL HARVEST MOON!" - and it was actually a clock on the side of a church.

Another time, I was about seventeen and I had one of them groups of mates where everyone actually hates each other, I was like the daft little mascot that says the funny things, I was like Phoebe from *Friends* only with less respect, and we were in a park snogging each other with mouths full of resentment and cheap cider, and I was over on the side being me and I saw on the ground a stunningly beautiful seashell, so I have a happy panic attack cos I think I'm looking at truth and beauty and I'm getting them all to come over and look at it, and then I realise that it isn't a stunningly beautiful seashell, it's the product of optimism, imagination and bad eyesight - it's a pile of sick, and I've been encouraging my friends to prod vomit.

I went home that night and got a binbag, and put in it all my teddies and childhood things, including optimism and imagination. I decided to be a grown up, I decided to be a cynic. No more duck trailing. The ducks can look after themselves.

[F/X: *Button Moon* theme tune fades out]

* * *

When I was four I found a purse, fake red leather, just £7 inside, the kind of purse a Mum has. When I was four the world was made out of Lego and the police station was square and certain. We handed the purse in and two months later they rang us and said that no one had claimed it, so I could have it, fake red leather with £7 inside.

When I was twenty-one the world was made of world and I was not square nor certain. When I was twenty-one I found a wallet and cut out the middle man.

"Find out what your defences are," she said being wise, on Facebook. That weekend she sat near a fire under the moon and being wise (on Facebook) she didn't put her hands in the fire, or reach for the moon.

I saw a teacher with a crocodile of kids in a park, she blew a whistle and they all went legging it to the slide, the swing, the seesaw, and one kid ran hard and wrong towards a bench, where he sat, beaming with his prize.

[F/X: Hospital monitors 'beep' in the background]

I had to go down to the operating theatre. This weird procedure, they try to get rid of all the blood clots with lasers. I had to lie flat on a metal table and stay very still.

The pain.

I bit through my tongue and my mouth filled with blood. I panicked.

I wanted my Dad to come and save me but I knew that he couldn't.

I made a decision.

I decided that no matter what happened, I'd make all of this into a good thing. Because otherwise this was just too shit. I would make something of this, I'd make this the making of me. I'd make me out of this.

If I could stay in that moment where the tennis ball reaches its height and takes a breath before remembering to fall, in that moment I'm wrapped in blankets, and safety smells of mustiness and Play-Doh.

[F/X: The theme tune to *'Allo 'Allo* plays quietly in the background]

I close my eyes and pretend I'm a tiny mouse curled up in a tramp's pocket, or that I'm seven and I still have that childhood sense of belonging, long before I knew it could get lost: I'm curled up on the couch with my Dad and we're watching our favourite programme which was *'Allo 'Allo* (which was set in the War, but I thought it was a programme about a load of nice people running a caff, I didn't notice the War).

[F/X: *'Allo 'Allo* theme tune fades out]

Me and my Dad were best friends then, but then I kept getting older, I couldn't help it, I started wearing lipstick and shouting, then I went away to university.

Everyone in Skem is pretty much the same; there's no class system, just people with slightly nicer shoes. So when I went to uni it was dead weird finding out that other people lived different. I'd never really thought about being working class, it had never come up in conversation, I'd just presumed that everyone lived in a council flat, because *doesn't the council own all buildings, just like they own fields and streets and air and sometimes they paint all the doors or put a new window in for Mary O'Hennessy who never misses Mass who's always getting her windows put through cos she doesn't give the ball back,* that's the way the world works! But all of a sudden, it wasn't. I started sitting in corners. Started shutting up. Remembered things I never knew, remembered 'Am I stupid?'. The library in Skem has pop-up books, the library there didn't know how to laugh.

Decide to lose my accent, leave it on the bus.

Then my Dad got sick.

It was the first time I'd seen him cry, the pain was in his foot. He got worse, they had to take his leg off, and then he had a stroke, and then—

(Jackie holds up a hankie that has 'My Dad Died' stitched onto it)

I guess Noel Edmonds was wrong.

I decided to cope by not coping. I decided to never think about him again. And that's what I did. Well, except for the annual bittersweet stab in the chest when Christmas shopping, and I'd spot good presents for him.

He used to tell me stories in primary colours because I was young and they were long ago. His hands, ground in dirt, filled in the gaps when he didn't know or have the breath for words. I was going to retell these stories when I was older. I would be an author, or a spaceman, or something. The stories were set in Liverpool, there was a gang like in *The Beano,* and a school... or something. I can't remember.

* * *

I'm back on the ward, shepherds pie and Jeremy Kyle, a jittery photocopy of normality, bravado wordsearch. We're waiting to find out if I'm gonna have to have anything cut off. The doctors don't know what's wrong with me, something vascular, something sudden, something girls in their thirties don't get, lots of tests, lots of posh frowning. My foot has gone black and wrong, not mine, I cover it up and ignore it.

(Jackie pulls out a notebook that says 'Facebook Statuses')

August 1st
Edna's off her tits on morphine, she just told me that in the war the women put gravy on their legs and the dogs licked it off.

August 13th
I'm copying Miles's coping methods. He says things like 'You live and learn', 'Onwards and upwards', 'You can only piss with the cock you've got'.

August 28th
Dr Quinn Medicine Woman comes and tells me that there's only one thing they can do other than cutting my leg off and you will not believe what it is. To get rid of the bacteria they want to put maggots on it. Dirty bastards! And the maggots are coming from Wales. I can imagine them all on their National Express coach with their little packed lunches, made-up to be coming to Manchester.

September 12th
There's a nurse here whose actual name is 'Sweetie'! Which is ironic, cos she's a bell-end.

September 20th
Dr Seuss came today and told me that the Welsh maggots haven't worked. In order to save my life they are going to amputate my leg, but don't worry, it'll be okay.

[F/X: A very loud mash-up of the theme tunes to *One Foot in the Grave* and *The Magic Roundabout* plays]

(This scene is a dream sequence. Jackie holds up a series of signs which read...)

This is a dream sequence.

I'm having my leg lopped off.

I'm going to show you what the world looks like with my eyes.

Please open your envelopes.

(Each member of the audience has an envelope containing a pair of light diffracting glasses which create a rainbow spectrum; it's pretty and trippy. If you have a pair, please wear them and look at something very bright, maybe wiggle about a bit - this will not recreate the dream sequence, but it will give you a taste of it. There is a dancing unicorn, lots of bubbles, and Jackie's glittery false leg is revealed)

Put on your special specs.

Good innit.

I know you have lost things, too.

(Jackie holds up a big ♥)

We'll be reet, eh?

You can take them off now...

If you want to.

Please don't nick them.

(Jackie uses sock puppets as the Welsh maggots)

Gareth Maggot: Oh well, I tried my best.

Barbara Maggot: Oh Gareth it's not your fault, we both tried us best luv, I ate as much of that minging foot as I could get down me.

Gareth Maggot: We shouldn't have had all those sandwiches on the coach here.

Barbara Maggot: It was a lovely day out tho', Manchester's lovely! Nice little wander round Primark, couple of galleries, eat a bit of foot.

Gareth Maggot: But that poor girl, wandering round with no leg.

Barbara Maggot: Oh she'll be fine Gareth. She's a bit of a weirdo anyway, it'll suit her, she might get more work now.

Gareth Maggot: She could be a paralympian.

[F/X: Hospital monitors 'beep' in the background]

Three things start happening when you have your leg off:

One - Everyone tells me I could be a paralympian. "Aye mate, and you could be an Olympian!"

Two - I keep getting called brave every five minutes, for anything, for eating a Twix, for going to the shop, and it's sort of patronising, you're being told you're brave for just continuing to exist, it's seen as quite offensive. However, I quite like compliments, so I think my position on the matter is: "How DARE you call me brave, but thanks for noticing I am rather aren't I!"

Three - Everyone asks me if it hurts to have your leg cut off. I try to sum up the exact pain with all my powers of language, it's this: "You know when you stub your toe?

Well fuck off."

My friends these days aren't the type who all hate each other, they're all good weirdoes, everyone I know now is Phoebe from *Friends*. They hum the theme tune to *One Foot in the Grave* and *Footloose*. Someone has made me a pirate costume. Someone has baked me a batch of gingerbread men with the right leg missing.

I'm alright, but then the pain and a nurse with a hen party for a face tells me about phantom pain. "The leg has gone, but your body thinks it's still there, so the pain stays, the same pain you had before."

What?!

That's stupid, who invented that? I ask her how long it takes to wear off and she says that it can last for the rest of your life.

I only let them cut it off so the pain would go.

For a while I don't cope. I throw in the towel. I can't deal with this for the rest of my life. I can't live on morphine. This isn't life.

Miles keeps coming in to see me even though I'm being a total bitch. Sometimes he comes and just holds my hand because there's nothing to say. I used to think that intimacy looked like red roses and Richard Curtis films and I didn't want that, I'm not Bridget Jones. But I was wrong, sometimes intimacy can look like a room you've been in for months that doesn't want to be a room anymore that smells of TCP and disabled cliché. After a week of being a dick I start telling myself, "You live and learn. Onwards and upwards. You can only piss with the cock you've got."

I might not have a leg or a Dad, but what I've always got is optimism, imagination, and a pen and paper, so, to cope, I start writing certificates for anyone, for anything that's good. I make one for a nurse who has one pretty ear, one for a doctor for giving me more time than I know he's got, one for a man for being really, really Welsh. When it gets harder I make them for people who have asymmetrical faces, odd socks, inappropriate eye contact, for having a head. I make one for Edna on how well she copes with hardship and she laughs at me, "You don't know the half of it love." I tell her I love her and she laughs again, "You haven't learnt love yet." I tell her I'm trying to be a grown up, and she teaches me to iron using a shoe.

I start to crave outdoors, I can smell the sky on people's skin when they come to visit. I become desperate to leave this hospital. I ask the nurse how long before I'll be able to walk and, more importantly, go up stairs. You see, I live in a flat above a shop. I've always hated it, it's just one in a long line of dodgy places I can only just afford that I'm totally not hard enough for. I live with a flatmate who smells like cheese and threadbare death. To get to my front door you have to run up these steps where the drug dealers meet their friends.

The nurse says: "Oh, it'll be about a year till you're back to normal. That's if it heals."

A year?

If it heals?

It turns out that my body isn't healing very well. It might not heal, and if that happens they'll have to cut off more, and if that doesn't heal then so on, and what, until I'm just a head? I totally lose my shit, I freak out, I'm a homeless amputee, that was not the plan, I was meant to be a spaceman.

They get me this social worker nurse with a strict hairstyle and a passive aggressive nose who tells me that I'll be able to get a council flat that's all adapted, a car and disability benefits.

Miles says I can stop at his for a bit, I don't tell him about the year thing cos I figure I'll get a flat soon enough, I mean, I have got one leg, surely the council will be nice.

I try every which way to get them to let me leave the hospital including pretending I have legal knowledge, throwing a tantrum, pointlessly throwing a ball of tissue paper at a doctor in frustration, but somehow it works, they let me leave.

On the way out of the hospital they give me a list of things to avoid. One of them is 'falling over'.

[F/X: Background sound of 'Lounge Jazz']

Miles's flat is dead grown up! His posters are in frames, he drinks wine out of - wine glasses! It's dead weird.

I can't believe how comfortable homes are, I have privacy for the first time in five months, I cry my minge clean off.

In physio I stand up for the first time, it hurts all over and feels like flying. I never thought I'd say this, but I have grown sick of being at the eye-line of people's arses.

If I get an infection or if I fall on my stump it might bugger it up and I'll have to have more amputated. I am thoroughly shitting myself. I draw secret, petrified graphs of when it should heal.

Life becomes a mess of forms, phone calls, physio and failure. The DSS make life hell for me. Hell. And I'm someone who genuinely finds having her leg off funny. I don't find the DSS funny. It's brutal, a total shambles, absurd and inhumane, and not in a good way.

I don't think I'm gonna get a council flat and I can't sponge off Miles forever, so I concoct a fairly rubbish plan - you know them magazines, *Take a Break* and *Chat* and *Pick Me Up*? The ones your Mum reads on the toilet? I sell a sensationalised version of this story to them all. *Chat* goes with 'Stumped? Not a chance!'. With the money I buy a little van and put a mattress in the back in case I need somewhere to live. I've started to lose my mind, to get by I eat a lot of shortbread.

Still not healed.

I feel really sad that Miles has never seen the best of me. We were together for five minutes and since then all he's seen is morphine and trauma. I haven't even had eyeliner on most of the time, I feel dead ashamed! All I want to do is impress him. But it's okay, I have a plan, all I need to do is be Superwoman.

Still haven't healed.

I embrace uncertainty, anxiety and pain. There's no special tactics, just a hopeful forging through - it's this light green sort of stoicism. I think about spring, change, and resilience. I think about new Mums and how they just get on with it, and I try not to drag anyone down whilst being mindful of doing healthy shit like putting my head under a blanket and crying, and then taking the blanket off and getting my shit together.

I learn the word 'debriding'. It's when, every other day, an angry Scottish woman uses tweezers to pull all the scabby mess out of your wound, and then they take a photo of it to send to some top doctor who will give you a verdict on how likely it is that they will cut more leg off. Shortbread, morphine, cope.

One day, I get up and there's little bits of paper all over the flat. I pick one up and it has a duck footprint drawn on it. I follow them round the flat and at the end is a fluffy toy duck with a note attached to its belly: *Jackie Hagan, stop trying to impress me, I was impressed from the beginning.*

I try trusting someone for the first time since my Dad died. I tell Miles what I've been scared of all along: I've been scared that I caused this; being a stress-head can cause blood clots, it's true, I've Googled it. He very gently tells me to stop Googling everything.

I start letting him help me with stuff. We untangle things together. I stop trying to be Superwoman. I let him know how much shortbread I've been on. I cry in front of him. Richard Curtis eat your heart out.

It's Christmas. Miles knows about the bittersweet stab in the chest of Christmas shopping and spotting good presents for people long gone. He's feels it, too. So we own it by naming it - it's called 'sweet cloddock'. That feels better, so we name some other shit:

Satisfleet: the satisfaction when you finally leave.

Dunnock: the fear that everyone will realise you are a child in grown up's clothing.

Hugglescoat: the desire to wake up as a little mouse curled up in a tramp's pocket.

Smoof: the soft appreciation of the moon and the sun in the sky at the same time. The phoenix that rises from the ashtray.

Higgleborry Meadow: the decision to smile; gob like a row of council houses, halfway houses and abandoned plots, for all the world to see.

Proud Bendish: inventing new words for the gaps you're going to own.

I'm worried that I've stressed my Mum out with it all. She's a Mum, all they want is for their kids to be safe and I haven't been, in the same way as my Dad wasn't, you know? I send her a text in the middle of the night: "I love you, I hope you're ok."

This is what she replies:

"You know your Aunty Jeanette has got a gastric band? Well, last week she caught a virus off the kids and got diarrhoea, and do you know where the poo came out? ... Her mouth, lol."

I'm starting to realise that I'm not quite as stupid as university taught me I was. I'm teaching Miles stuff. Things like:

One - No one looks like Kate Moss, including Kate Moss.

Two - Romanticise the repetitive clunk.

Three - Give your pets a heroic aura.

Four - The fight for sexual equality is not between men and women, it's between people and dickheads.

Five - You're probably not as ugly as you think you are, you are a generous buffet of crisps.

Six - The minimum fill line on a kettle... is real.

Me and Miles start pestering the DSS and eventually, after ages, we get me a council flat with a ramp. It's the size of a postage stamp and I am made-up. I decorate it like a disco forest grotto circus rocket; it's beautiful, it gives other people a migraine, but I think it looks like the inside of my mind. I'm so happy to live somewhere that's mine, it's even got central heating. When I can't sleep for the pain I just look at my flat and it feels worth it. I think the reason I was in and out of psychiatric ward in my twenties was because I wouldn't face pain, I wouldn't trust anyone and I could never afford somewhere to live that was okay, and safe.

We finally find out what's wrong with me, it's called Systemic Sclerosis and it's shit, it's a life-limiting auto-immune disease, it's the type of thing you just don't wanna Google.

I learn to walk bit by bit, first it's using bars, then crutches, then sticks, then one stick, then none. It hurts, but everything hurts now, so I'm just really strict with my head, I don't allow self-pity for a second. When people are annoying me, moaning about their stubbed toe or their mansion's too big or whatever, I imagine I'm a Care Bear and exude love for them out of my fluffy belly, while not listening to what they're saying. I notice nice things a lot. I nurture positivity, whilst remaining a bit of a sarcastic git.

Still not healed.

I think me and Miles might be solid. I do know that I'm not gonna be a normal girlfriend. I don't have long brown hair and outfits I think the boys will like. I'm not pretty, I'm just something, unapologetically me.

I don't know how to do life or love, but I remembered something my Dad taught me when I was growing up:

"What do you do if you don't know something? Make it up."

(Jackie sits down on the edge of the stage in a spotlight. She holds up a teddy with colourful hair, it has one leg. She makes it clear it represents her. She holds up a big Care Bear, it has one leg. She uses them as puppets in the following...)

Jackie Teddybear: Ey! I've got something to tell you!

Care Bear: What? You forgot about me for a bit didn't you. It's alright kid, I've been up here having a pint with God.

Jackie Teddybear: Daaad! You're not in heaven, you're in my head!

Care Bear: Whatever you say Buggerlugs. So you don't believe in God anymore, eh? I remember when you used to do your little prayers - "Ey! Lord! Make that fella from Take That kiss me!"

Jackie Teddybear: Shurrruuup! His name was Mark Owen *actually*... Dad, I've missed you.

Care Bear: Sorry luv.

Jackie Teddybear: No... don't say sorry, not sorry.

[F/X: The theme tune to *'Allo 'Allo* begins quietly in the background]

Care Bear: Ey, stop your rambling now you, our programme's on.

(They watch *'Allo 'Allo* for a bit)

Jackie Teddybear: Dad? You know in *'Allo 'Allo*? Was there a war on?!

Care Bear: Yeah! But it's alright, we won. Ey, I'm proud of you, you know.

Jackie Teddybear: Yeah, I'm proud of me, too.

On March 12th 2014 the nurse says to me, "Your stump is a funny shape, but that's just cos it healed weird."

It's healed weird.

It's *healed*.

That means I'm not having anything else amputated! Then she says, "Do you want to look at it?"

"Naaah! I'm alright, I've just eaten."

And she leaves me alone with it.

* * *

Uh oh. The word 'stump'. Minging innit. Absurd innit. Sort of forthright and funny. Everyone suggests alternatives cos no one can deal with it.

'Leglet', hmm, a bit Winnie the Pooh, get a grip, embarrassing. 'Residual limb', makes me think of blocked-up drains. Someone suggests I just call it John, which is nice, except, well, that was the Elephant Man's name wasn't it, no offence mate! Don't wanna create an Elephant Man in the room. Someone suggests Bert, which sort of fits, you don't expect a Bert to be pretty; "Don't mind Bert, he always eats with his hands." Berts wear flat-caps and call a spade a spade. Huh, call a spade a spade, yeah, call a stump a stump.

The word 'stump'. Minging innit. Absurd innit. Sort of forthright and funny. Could have been my middle name. Proper fits what it is. Stump.

Say it with me: "Stump!"

Right, should we look at you then?

(Jackie peeks inside the bandages)

Urrrgh, God! You know the blonde one out of *Birds of a Feather*? It looks like her miserable gob! Right, how to deal with this, could hide it away forever, or...

(Jackie gets a marker pen out and draws eyes on the stump)

"Miles! I've got something to tell yer!"

(Jackie uses stump as a puppet and says in a daft voice...)

"We're not gorra have anything else amputated."

(Jackie pours champagne into her false leg and downs it all)

When things get hard I do this: I think of things that I'm grateful for 24/7:

Mancs, Scousers, tea, coffee, swearing, toddlers, jumble sales, wisdom, my tattoos, my hair, my face, me, and above all, nurses.

I can't bring myself to be grateful for Noel Edmonds.

1.
CELEBRITY STUMPS

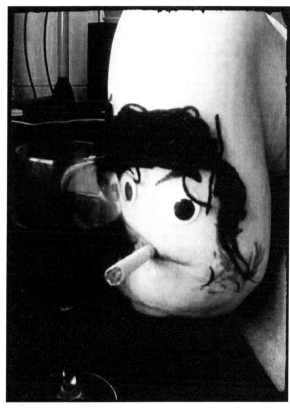

GUESS MY STUMP

2.

CELEBRITY STUMPS

GUESS MY STUMP

3.
CELEBRITY STUMPS

GUESS MY STUMP

4.
CELEBRITY STUMPS

GUESS MY STUMP

5.

CELEBRITY STUMPS

GUESS MY STUMP

Answers:
1. Dylan Moran; 2. Harry Potter;
3. David Bowie; 4. Marilyn Monroe;
5. The man from the *Go Compare* adverts.